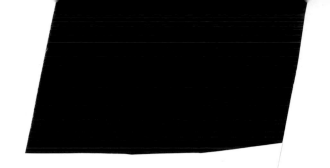

Flippers and Fins™

Swimming with Dolphins

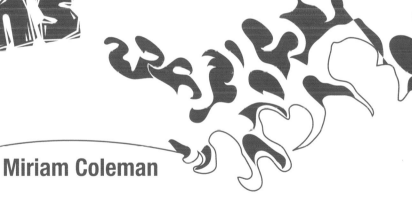

Miriam Coleman

PowerKiDS
press™

New York

Published in 2010 by The Rosen Publishing Group, Inc.
29 East 21st Street, New York, NY 10010

First Edition

Editor: Joanne Randolph
Book Design: Greg Tucker
Photo Researcher: Jessica Gerweck

Photo Credits: Cover © Stephen Frink/zefa/Corbis; p. 5 Shutterstock.com; p. 7 © Craig Tuttle/Corbis; p. 9 © Juniors Bildarchiv/age fotostock; p. 11 Jeff Foott/Getty Images; p. 13 © Staffan Widstrand/Corbis; pp. 15, 19 © Jeffrey L. Rotman/Corbis; p. 17 George Lepp/Getty Images; p. 21 © Denis Scott/Corbis.

Library of Congress Cataloging-in-Publication Data

Coleman, Miriam.
    Swimming with dolphins / Miriam Coleman. — 1st ed.
        p. cm. — (Flippers and fins)
    Includes index.
    ISBN 978-1-4042-8090-8 (library binding) — ISBN 978-1-4358-3237-4 (pbk.) —
ISBN 978-1-4358-3238-1 (6-pack)
    1. Dolphins—Juvenile literature. I. Title.
    QL737.C432C565 2010
    599.53—dc22
                                            2008051916

Manufactured in the United States of America

Contents

Meet the Dolphin

If you go on a boat ride in the ocean, you might see some large fish jumping out of the water around the boat. These large, jumping fish may not be fish at all. They might be dolphins. Dolphins live in oceans all over the world. They are playful sea animals that love to **surf** on ocean waves. Dolphins sometimes follow boats so that they can ride in the waves the boats make.

Sailors have long believed that seeing these friendly animals swimming beside their ships is good luck. Ancient Greeks put pictures of dolphins on their coins and pottery. Read on to find out more about dolphins!

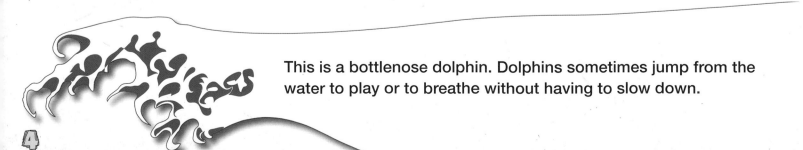

This is a bottlenose dolphin. Dolphins sometimes jump from the water to play or to breathe without having to slow down.

Dolphins Are Not Fish

   Dolphins swim in the sea, but they are not fish. Dolphins are mammals, as people, horses, and cats are.

   Fish breathe through gills, but mammals, such as dolphins, have lungs to breathe air. Fish are cold blooded, which means that their body **temperatures** change with their surroundings. Dolphins and other mammals are warm blooded and make their own heat. Their body temperatures are always the same. Fish lay eggs, but dolphins, like most mammals, give birth to live babies. Dolphins feed their babies with milk from their bodies, something only mammals can do.

Dolphins are part of a group of animals called cetaceans. They are related to whales and porpoises.

So Many Dolphins

Dolphins that live in the ocean are called marine dolphins. There are 33 different **species** of marine dolphins. The most famous is the bottlenose dolphin. It lives in warm, **tropical** waters, often close to shore. It has gray skin and can grow to be 12 feet (4 m) long. The orca is the largest dolphin, growing to be 29 feet (9 m) long.

River dolphins live in freshwater. They can be found in muddy rivers and lakes in China, India, and South America. River dolphins are smaller than marine dolphins, and their noses are much longer. There are only five different species of river dolphins.

This is a kind of marine dolphin, called Risso's dolphin. This dolphin generally swims in deep waters away from the shore.

Fins, Flippers, and Flukes

Dolphins are great swimmers. They have **sleek** bodies that are shaped to cut quickly through the water. Some dolphins can swim over 20 miles per hour (32 km/h).

A dolphin's body shape is only part of the reason dolphins are so fast in the water. Dolphins have powerful fins on their tails, called flukes. They move these up and down to push their bodies forward. Most dolphins have a fin on their backs, called a dorsal fin. The dorsal fin keeps the dolphin steady while it swims. Dolphins also have flippers on the sides of their bodies. The flippers help dolphins turn and stop while they swim.

You can see the flukes and flippers on these Atlantic spotted dolphins. Dolphins use their flukes to jump out of the water.

Breathing in the Sea

Dolphins spend their lives in the water, but they still need to breathe air. Dolphins have lungs, as people do, but they do not breathe through their mouths or noses. Instead, a dolphin breathes through a blowhole on top of its head.

A blowhole is a kind of nostril, like you have on your nose. When the dolphin is underwater, the blowhole stays tightly closed. When dolphins come to the **surface**, strong **muscles** open the blowhole so the dolphins can draw in air. Dolphins can hold their breath for a long time under water, but they usually come up for air two or three times a minute.

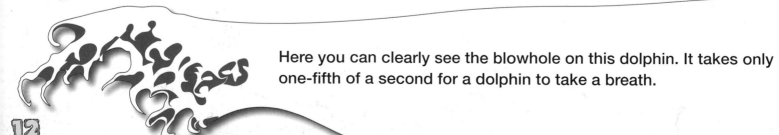

Here you can clearly see the blowhole on this dolphin. It takes only one-fifth of a second for a dolphin to take a breath.

Baby Dolphins

Dolphins usually give birth to just one baby at a time. The mother carries the baby inside her body for about 12 months before giving birth. The baby is called a calf. Its fins are very soft and **flexible**. Dolphins are born underwater. As soon as it is born, a dolphin calf swims to the top of the water to take a breath of air.

For the first few months of life, dolphin mothers nurse the calves with milk and keep them safe. When the calf grows older, the mother will teach it to catch its own fish. In some species of dolphins, the babies stay with their mothers their whole lives.

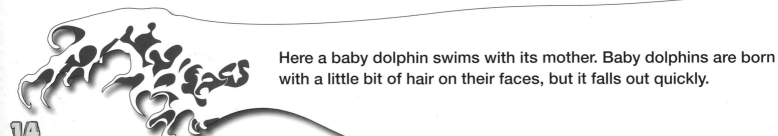

Here a baby dolphin swims with its mother. Baby dolphins are born with a little bit of hair on their faces, but it falls out quickly.

Working Together

Most types of dolphins live and travel in groups. Groups of 10 to 20 dolphins are called pods. Some kinds of dolphins even live in herds of 100 to 1,000.

Dolphins in the pod help each other. They tell each other if food is nearby and work together to catch it. They tell each other when there is danger and **protect** other dolphins that are hurt.

Dolphins talk to each other by making different sounds. They **whistle**, bark, click, and squeak. They make these sounds by pushing air in and out from special sacs below their blowholes.

Common dolphins, like these, swim in pods of hundreds, or even thousands. They swim fast and work together to herd and catch fish.

Time for Dinner

Dolphins are carnivores, which means they eat meat. They have sharp cone-shaped teeth and they are skillful hunters. Dolphins like to eat fish, squid, lobsters, shrimp, and crabs. River dolphins also eat turtles. Larger dolphins, such as killer whales, eat sharks, seals, otters, and smaller dolphins.

Dolphins do not have muscles to chew their food. Instead, they swallow it whole. If a fish is too large, the dolphin will shake it or rub it on the ocean floor until smaller pieces break off.

Dolphins often hunt together. A group of dolphins will herd schools of fish together to make them easier to catch.

This dolphin has caught an octopus for its dinner. Dolphins use sounds to help them find food underwater.

Dolphins for Dinner

Adult dolphins are fast and strong, so they have few natural **predators**. Baby dolphins are easier to catch. Some large sharks, such as tiger sharks, bull sharks, and great white sharks, are good at hunting adult dolphins. Dolphins often have **scars** on their bodies from shark bites. Killer whales also eat smaller species of dolphins.

People once hunted dolphins to eat their meat and make leather from their skin. They would also use oil from dolphins for lamps and cooking. People do not often hunt dolphins today.

Great white sharks, like this one, sometimes hunt dolphins. Dolphins may try to fight off sharks, but no one knows for sure.

People and Dolphins

Dolphins are smart and friendly animals. Bottlenose dolphins can learn to do tricks and play games. They can often be seen at aquariums and zoos. Some dolphins have been known to save people from sharks or from drowning.

Sometimes people's actions can hurt dolphins, though. Some fishermen use large nets to catch food like tuna and shrimp. They often catch and kill dolphins, too. **Pollution** also hurts dolphins, making their water unsafe to live in or killing the fish they need to eat. We must protect the waters where dolphins live so that we do not hurt these amazing animals.

Glossary

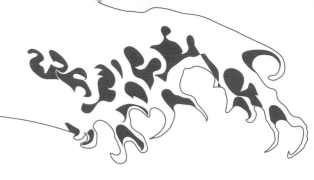

flexible (FLEK-sih-bul) Moving and bending in many ways.

muscles (MUH-sulz) Parts of the body under the skin that make the body move.

pollution (puh-LOO-shun) Man-made waste that hurts Earth's air, land, or water.

predators (PREH-duh-terz) Animals that kill other animals for food.

protect (pruh-TEKT) To keep safe.

scars (SKARZ) Marks left by healed cuts.

sleek (SLEEK) Even and smooth on the outside.

species (SPEE-sheez) One kind of living thing. All people are one species.

surf (SURF) To ride on ocean waves.

surface (SER-fes) The outside of anything.

temperatures (TEM-pur-churz) The heat in living bodies.

tropical (TRAH-puh-kul) Having to do with the warm parts of Earth that are near the equator.

whistle (WIH-sul) To make a high, clear sound by blowing through the lips or teeth.

Index

A
animals, 4, 22

B
boat, 4
bodies, 6, 10, 20

D
danger, 16

F
fish, 4, 6, 14, 18, 22

M
muscles, 12, 18

O
ocean(s), 4, 8

P
pollution, 22
predators, 20

R
ride, 4

S
scars, 20
species, 8, 14, 20

T
temperatures, 6

W
water(s), 4, 8, 10, 12, 14, 22
world, 4

Web Sites

Due to the changing nature of Internet links, PowerKids Press has developed an online list of Web sites related to the subject of this book. This site is updated regularly. Please use this link to access the list:
www.powerkidslinks.com/ffin/dolphin/